Making Smart Choices

LUCIA RAATMA

Children's Press®
An Imprint of Scholastic Inc.
New York Toronto London Auckland Sydney
Mexico City New Delhi Hong Kong
Danbury, Connecticut

Content Consultants

Dave Riley, PhD, is a professor in the Human Development & Family Studies Department at the University of Wisconsin–Madison. Colette Sisco is a faculty member in the psychology department at Madison College, Madison, Wisconsin.

Library of Congress Cataloging-in-Publication Data

Raatma, Lucia.
 Making smart choices/by Lucia Raatma.
    p. cm. — (A true book)
 Includes bibliographical references and index.
 ISBN 978-0-531-25524-7 (lib. bdg.) — ISBN 978-0-531-23924-7 (pbk.)
1. Health—Juvenile literature. 2. Health behavior in children—Juvenile literature. 3. Choice (Psychology) in children—Juvenile literature. 4. Decision making in children—Juvenile literature.
I. Title.
 RA777.R32 2013
 613—dc23   2012036005

All rights reserved. Published in 2013 by Children's Press, an imprint of Scholastic Inc.
Printed in the United States of America 113
SCHOLASTIC, CHILDREN'S PRESS, A TRUE BOOK™, and associated logos are trademarks and/or registered trademarks of Scholastic Inc.
1 2 3 4 5 6 7 8 9 10 R 22 21 20 19 18 17 16 15 14 13

Front cover: Child jumping a bicycle over ramp and friends

Back cover: USDA MyPlate illustration for a healthy meal

Find the Truth!

Everything you are about to read is true *except* for one of the sentences on this page.

Which one is **TRUE**?

T or F There are different kinds of carbohydrates. Some are good for your body.

T or F Most kids only need an hour or two of exercise each week.

Find the answers in this book.

3

Contents

THE BIG TRUTH!

Only You Can Make Your Own Choices

4

A boy and his mother prepare a healthy meal.

4 Handling Stress

What choices can help you feel better? **37**

Eating fruits and vegetables is always a good choice. ⟹

What sorts of choices have you made today?

CHAPTER 1

Taking Time for Choices

You make choices every day. Should you wear a blue shirt or a red shirt? Do you want a vanilla milk shake or a chocolate milk shake? Some of the choices you make are pretty easy. But others are hard. Some choices can affect your life in serious ways. Remember that whatever your options are, you control the choice.

People will try to help you, but your final choices are up to you.

Making Choices at Home

When you're at home, you're faced with many choices. Should you play a game with your younger brother or study for your math test? Both choices are good ones. But if your math test is tomorrow, that might be more important. You will have another chance to play with your brother. But you won't have another chance to study for your test.

Try studying for tests and completing your homework right when you get home from school. There might be time to play a game after you're done.

Make sure you complete any home chores assigned to you.

Should you walk the dog or watch your favorite show on TV? If walking the dog is your responsibility, it's important to follow through. Your parents are expecting you to do it. Your pet is relying on you, too. You can watch the TV show when you get back. You could also record it for later.

If your friend is counting on you, make sure you're there to help.

Making Choices With Friends

Sometimes you may be faced with hard choices that have to do with friends. Maybe you have promised to help your best friend babysit on Friday night. But then you get invited to a party. What do you do? Think about how much your friend means to you. Remember that you made a promise. How would you feel if your friend broke a promise to you?

What if a friend wants you to do something dangerous? Maybe he wants you to swim with him in his family's pool when no one else is home. You know an adult should be watching you. Do you choose to swim? Or do you say "no thanks"? What if you or your friend got hurt with no adults around? If a friend pressures you to do something dangerous, maybe he isn't such a good friend.

If you go swimming, it's important to have an adult there to keep an eye on you.

Getting Help With Choices

As you grow up, you may feel pressure from all sides. Your parents may want you to do certain things. But your friends may want you to do something else. It can be hard to weigh all your options and know which one is right. Sometimes it helps to make a list of all the pros and cons for a choice you have to make.

Writing down an issue's pros and cons can help you think through an important decision.

It sometimes helps to hear another person's opinion about an issue.

If a choice is really hard, it helps to talk about it. Find someone you trust and talk through the choice. This person could be an older brother or sister, a parent, an aunt or uncle, a guidance counselor, or a friend. Make sure it's someone who wants what is best for you. It can be helpful to discuss all your worries with another person.

CHAPTER 2

Making Good Food Choices

What do you put in your body each day? Remember that food is fuel for your body. It affects how much energy you have and how good you feel. Are you starting your day with a sugary cereal? Do you drink soda all day? Take a look at what you are eating and see how your body reacts.

 Thirsty? Nothing is better for you than plain water.

What Is Protein?

Proteins are building blocks that keep your body strong. If you exercise a lot, protein helps your muscles recover and grow stronger. Protein is in meat, beans, milk products, eggs, tofu, and nuts. It is also in rice, bread, and vegetables in smaller amounts.

Not all cholesterol comes from food. Your body makes some of its own cholesterol.

Nuts such as walnuts are a great source of protein.

Some sources of protein are better than others. For instance, a serving of grilled chicken has fewer **calories** and less fat than a greasy cheeseburger. Proteins that come from animals, such as meat, eggs, and whole milk, have **cholesterol**. Other proteins, such as beans, nuts, and tofu, do not. Start learning how to read labels for the foods you eat. Use these labels to see how much protein you eat each day.

It's best to eat fruits and vegetables in a variety of colors. Then you get a wider mix of nutrients.

What Are Carbohydrates?

Foods that come from plants contain **carbohydrates**. Carbohydrates change into fuel that gives your body energy. There are two major kinds of carbohydrates: complex and simple. Complex carbohydrates are better for your body than simple carbohydrates. Complex carbohydrates are found in fruits, vegetables, whole wheat bread, and brown rice. These foods are also high in **fiber**, which helps your body run smoothly.

Foods such as white bread, cookies, doughnuts, and candy contain simple carbohydrates. Foods with simple carbohydrates are often highly processed and contain added sugar. Want to make the best carbohydrate choices? Choose foods that are closer to nature. Fresh strawberries are better than strawberry ice cream. Hot oatmeal is better than an oatmeal cookie.

The average American eats 156 pounds (71 kilograms) of sugar each year!

Jelly beans and other candies might be fruit flavored, but they are not nearly as good for you as real, unprocessed fruits.

Is Fat Good or Not?

You might think that all fat is gross and not good for you. But that's not true. Some fats in food help your body stay healthy. For instance, fat from eggs and olive oil can be good for you in small amounts. But other processed fats, often found in things like margarine and cookies, are not healthy at all.

Eggs contain a lot of important nutrients, including good fats.

Processed sugar is okay in small amounts.

What About Sugar?

Everyone enjoys an occasional treat. What's a birthday without cake or Thanksgiving without pie? But remember that sweets are best when they are saved for special days. Sugar gives you energy at first, but then it makes you feel lazy and tired. If you eat and drink a lot of sugar every day, you may gain weight and feel terrible. If you gain too much weight, you may become overweight, or obese.

Ask a parent to show you some ways of making your fruits and vegetables taste great. You can also look for recipes online or at the library.

Making Good Meal Choices

If you're like most people, you probably eat three meals a day and maybe a snack. When you make your food choices, take a minute to think. Ask yourself, "Is this the healthiest option for my body?" and "How will I feel later?" French fries may smell great, but a side of mixed vegetables will better fuel your body.

Does Your Plate Look Like MyPlate?

The U.S. Department of Agriculture's MyPlate illustration shows what a nutritious meal should look like. One-quarter of the plate is lean protein. Another quarter of the plate is whole grains. One-half of the plate is fruits and vegetables. A serving of dairy is off to the side.

Look at your next meal. Does it look like MyPlate? Many people don't eat enough fruits and vegetables. But these foods provide important **vitamins** and **minerals**. Can you make your next meal look like MyPlate?

Only You Can Make Your Own Choices

As you grow up, you'll be faced with more and more choices. Some are not so important. Others can affect your health, your schoolwork, and your relationships with people. See if you can learn to make good choices every day.

You're hungry. Should you choose an apple or a chocolate bar?

You're thirsty. Should you reach for your water bottle or have a soda?

You don't have any homework today. Should you play a computer game at home or join your friends for a game of kickball?

School is done for the day. Should you go to soccer practice or skip it and hang out with your friends?

It's great to go outside and play, especially when the weather is nice.

CHAPTER 3

Making a Choice to Be Active

What is your typical day like? Do you take a car or a bus everywhere? Do you relax in front of the TV after school? Do you walk to and from school and play outside when you get home? The answers to these questions help show how active you are. And the more active you are, the healthier and happier you'll be.

Exercise can improve your mood.

Finding Hobbies You Like

When you're not at school or doing chores at home, what do you like to do? What activity makes you feel happy and energized? If you don't have a few fun hobbies, explore some that you might like. Maybe you enjoy swimming. Or maybe you are interested in taking a karate class.

Karate and other types of classes are a good way to get moving and make some friends.

Having a hobby you enjoy can be relaxing.

Bird-watching can be a relaxing outdoor activity.

Having special hobbies is important for a happy life. If you have a passion for tennis, work hard at improving your game. If you love bird-watching, learn everything you can about the birds in your area. If you enjoy running, get a stopwatch and see how fast you can go. When you choose to be active, your life will be full and fun.

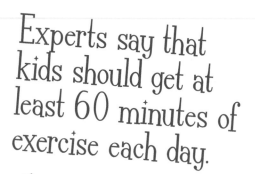

Experts say that kids should get at least 60 minutes of exercise each day.

It can be good to relax sometimes, but make sure you turn off the TV and get moving for a while every day!

Getting Up and Moving

It can be tempting to spend hours in front of the TV or computer. There are probably many shows you like to watch and games you like to play. But sometimes it's important to turn off the TV and computer. Staring at a screen all day is not good for your eyes or your mood. You'll feel better if you get up and move.

When you stay seated for a long period of time, your body feels it. You can get stiff, and you don't burn many calories. If you stay still too often, you might start gaining weight. You also might not have much energy. So get outside and break a sweat. Go for a bike ride or a walk or a run. Is the weather bad? You can get moving inside by playing a Wii or Kinect video game.

Riding bikes with your friends gives you a chance to use some energy and socialize.

Exercising With Friends

You probably like spending time with friends. There are lots of different things you can do. Instead of playing computer games when you get together, head outside to play tag or hide-and-seek. You could take your dog for a walk. Or maybe you could go to the local playground.

Making Smart Choices Timeline

1956

The President's Council on Youth Fitness, now called the President's Council on Fitness, Sports, and Nutrition, is founded.

1983

The Drug Abuse Resistance Education (DARE) program is founded. Members of this group may have visited your school.

For something more planned, sign up for activities that both you and a friend like. Maybe you could take a dance or karate class together. Perhaps you could go on a nature hike at your local park on the weekend. Or maybe you both could try horseback riding. You can make the choice to be active and enjoy being with your friends at the same time.

2007
The National Football League creates NFL Play 60, a program that encourages physical fitness and nutrition for kids.

2011
The U.S. Department of Agriculture adopts the MyPlate guidelines.

Joining a Team

Another great way to stay active is to join a sports team. You could try baseball, softball, or soccer. Other options are football, basketball, and swimming. Talk to your parents and find out what your community offers. By joining a team, you have regular practices and games or competitions. You will also make friends along the way.

There are a lot of different sports out there. Try out some sports you might be interested in. Which ones are right for you?

When you're part of a team, your teammates and coach are counting on you.

Remember that when you join a team, you make a commitment. You are responsible for attending practices and games. You are expected to listen to your coaches and try your best. Joining a team is often a good choice to make. And you might just find a sport that you love and will want to keep playing your whole life.

It is important to
find healthy ways
to handle stress.

Handling Stress

Some days, everything seems to go your way. You get an A on your science test. Your best friend invites you for a sleepover. You are chosen for the school play. Other days, everything seems to go against you. Maybe you failed a test or your best friend is mad at you. You may feel upset and angry. How do you deal with that **stress**?

Too much stress can give you a stomachache or a headache.

Food and Stress

When you are feeling stressed out, there is one important thing to remember. Food will not make you feel better. So don't reach for a bag of chips or a gallon of ice cream. Junk food might taste good now, but in a little while, your energy will suddenly drop. You'll end up feeling stuffed, tired, and still stressed out.

Experts believe that listening to music can fight stress.

Fried foods generally contain a lot of calories, but not much nutrition.

Try going for a jog with your family or friends.

Exercise and Stress

Unlike food, exercise will actually make you feel better when you're upset. If something is bothering you, a walk or bike ride may be just what you need. It will help you clear your mind and burn off some energy. When you're done, your problem might not seem so bad. Or you may be able to think about it more clearly.

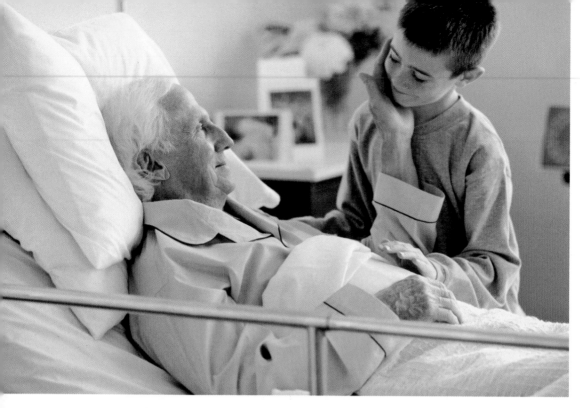

When a family member is sick, it can be very stressful. Don't be afraid to ask an adult or a friend for help when you need it.

Asking for Help

As you grow older, you may face problems that are very difficult to deal with. Maybe your parents tell you they are getting a divorce. Maybe you are being bullied at school. Or maybe someone close to you is very sick. At times like these, it is important to make good choices and decisions.

One good choice is to find someone to talk to. This might be a trusted friend or family member. You could also talk to a professional counselor or **psychologist**. Talking through your worries can help you feel better. It can also help you look at a problem in a new way. Maybe a solution will be easier to see.

Sometimes just sharing your worries with someone can help you feel a little better.

It is important to think for yourself. A friend who wants you to do something dangerous or illegal may not be a friend at all.

Peer Pressure

One of the hardest things you'll have to deal with is peer pressure. Peer pressure happens when people your age encourage you to do things that you shouldn't do. Maybe a group of kids wants you to cheat on a test. Or maybe they dare you to steal something from a store. Remember that only you can make your own choices. You always have the power to say no. ★

Saying No to Drugs and Alcohol

Some kids who are unhappy or worried turn to drugs or alcohol. However, drugs and alcohol are not healthy. They can damage your body, and you can become **addicted** to them.

If anyone offers you drugs or alcohol, say no. It may be hard to do, but trust yourself. Anyone who wants you to try drugs or alcohol is not really your friend. Find someone to talk to. Look for other ways to handle the problems you're facing.

True Statistics

Number of minutes kids should be active each day: 60

Number of hours that most kids spend with TVs, computers, and video games each day: Almost 8

Number of calories that kids ages 9 to 13 should consume each day: 1,600 to 2,600 (depending on activity level)

Number of calories in a Big Mac, large fries, and small Coke: 1,200

Number of calories a 75-pound (34 kg) kid burns in an hour of swimming at a moderate pace: 300

Did you find the truth?

T There are different kinds of carbohydrates. Some are good for your body.

F Most kids only need an hour or two of exercise each week.

Resources

Books

Culbert, Timothy, and Rebecca Kajander. *Be the Boss of Your Stress*. Minneapolis: Free Spirit Publishing, 2007.

Hardyman, Robyn. *Healthy Bodies*. New York: PowerKids Press, 2012.

Kajander, Rebecca, and Timothy Culbert. *Be Fit, Be Strong, Be You*. Minneapolis: Free Spirit Publishing, 2010.

Visit this Scholastic Web site for more information on making smart choices:
★ www.factsfornow.scholastic.com
Enter the keywords **Making Smart Choices**

Important Words

addicted (uh-DIKT-id) — unable to give up doing or using something

calories (KAL-uh-reez) — measurements of the amount of energy contained in food

carbohydrates (kar-buh-HYE-drates) — substances in food such as bread, rice, and potatoes that give you energy

cholesterol (kuh-LESS-tuh-rawl) — a fatty substance that humans and animals need to digest food and produce certain vitamins; too much can lead to heart disease

fiber (FYE-bur) — a part of fruits, vegetables, and grains that passes through the body but is not digested

minerals (MIN-ur-uhlz) — solid substances that are found in the earth and in food, and that help keep your body healthy

proteins (PROH-teenz) — substances found in all living plant and animals cells

psychologist (sye-KAH-luh-jist) — a person who studies people's minds and emotions and the ways that people behave

stress (STRESS) — mental or emotional strain or pressure

vitamins (VYE-tuh-minz) — substances in food that are necessary for good health

Index

Page numbers in **bold** indicate illustrations.

About the Author

Lucia Raatma is a writer and editor who enjoys working on books for young readers. She earned a bachelor's degree in English from the University of South Carolina and a master's degree in cinema studies from New York University. She likes writing about all sorts of subjects including history, conservation, wildlife, character education, and social media. She lives with her husband and their two children in the Tampa Bay area of Florida.

[5]